TAKE TEN YEARS

Published by Evans Brothers Limited
2A Portman Mansions
Chiltern Street
London W1U 6NR

© Evans Brothers Limited 1992

First published 1992
© in this edition 1996
Reprinted 1998, 1999, 2001

Typeset by Fleetlines Typesetters, Southend-on-Sea
Printed in Spain by GRAFO, S.A. - Bilbao

ISBN 0 237 51682 9

Acknowledgements

Maps – Jillian Luff of Bitmap Graphics
Design – Neil Sayer
Editor – Caroline Sheldrick

For permission to reproduce copyright material the author and
publishers gratefully acknowledge the following:

Cover photographs – (top row) NASA/Topham, Hulton Picture
Company, (middle row) Popperfoto, (bottom row) Popperfoto,
Topham, Hulton Picture Company. Page 4 – (from top) Associated
Press/Topham, Topham, Associated Press/Topham, Topham,
Popperfoto; page 5 – (from top) Alex Webb/Magnum, Popperfoto,
Popperfoto, Topham, Alexander Tsiaras/Science Photo Library;
page 8 – (left, right) Popperfoto; page 9 – Popperfoto; page 10 –
(top) Stevenson/Retna, (bottom) Popperfoto; page 11 – (left)
Popperfoto, (right) Topham; page 12 – Popperfoto; page 14 – (top)
Novosti Press Agency/Science Photo Library, (bottom left)
Popperfoto, (bottom right) The Hulton Picture Company; page 15 –
Topham; page 16 – The Hulton Picture Company; page 17 –
Associated Press/Topham; page 18 – Popperfoto; page 19 – (left)
ECOSCENE/Platt, (right) Popperfoto; page 20 (left) Costa Manos/
Magnum; page 21 – (top) Popperfoto, (bottom left) Associated
Press/Topham, (bottom right) Topham; page 22 – Topham; page 23
– (left) Associated Press/Topham, (right) The Hulton Picture
Company; page 24 – (top) Michael Putland/Retna, (middle) The
Hulton Picture Company, (bottom) Popperfoto; page 26 –
Associated Press/Topham; page 27 – (top) The Hulton Picture
Company, (bottom) Popperfoto; page 28 – (top) Robert Harding
Picture Library, (bottom) Topham; page 29 – Popperfoto; page 30 –
(top, bottom) Popperfoto; page 31 – (top) NASA/Science Photo
Library, (left) AllSport/Tony Duffy; page 32 – Popperfoto; page 33
(top) Popperfoto, (bottom) The Hulton Picture Company; page 34 –
(top) Associated Press/Topham, (bottom left) Popperfoto, (bottom
right) Lucasfilms Ltd/BFI Stills, Posters and Designs; page 35 –
Associated Press/Topham; page 36 – (top) The Hulton Picture
Company, (bottom) Popperfoto; page 37 – (top) Popperfoto,
(bottom) AllSport/Tony Duffy; page 38 – Popperfoto; page 39 –
(left) Alexander Tsiaras/Science Photo Library, (right) Popperfoto;
page 40 – (left) The Hulton Picture Company, (right) Harmon/
Magnum; page 41 – (top) Barnaby's Picture Library, (bottom)
Popperfoto; page 42 – (left) Topham, (right) Associated Press/
Topham; page 43 (top, bottom) Associated Press/Topham; page 44
– (from top) Renee Lynn/Science Photo Library, Alfred Pasieka/
Science Photo Library, Simon Fraser/Science Photo Library, Heini
Schneebeli/Science Photo Library, Peter Aprahamian/Science Photo
Library; page 45 – Martin Dohrn/Science Photo Library, David
Parker/Science Photo Library, NASA/Science Photo Library,
Paramount Pictures/BFI Stills, Posters and Designs, Steve Percival/
Science Photo Library.

TAKE TEN YEARS
1970s

CLINT TWIST

EVANS BROTHERS LIMITED

Contents

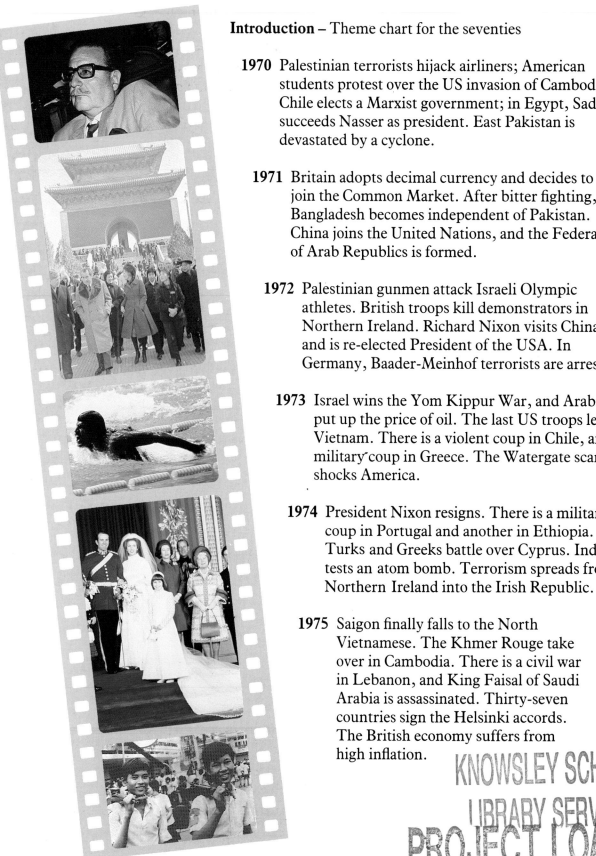

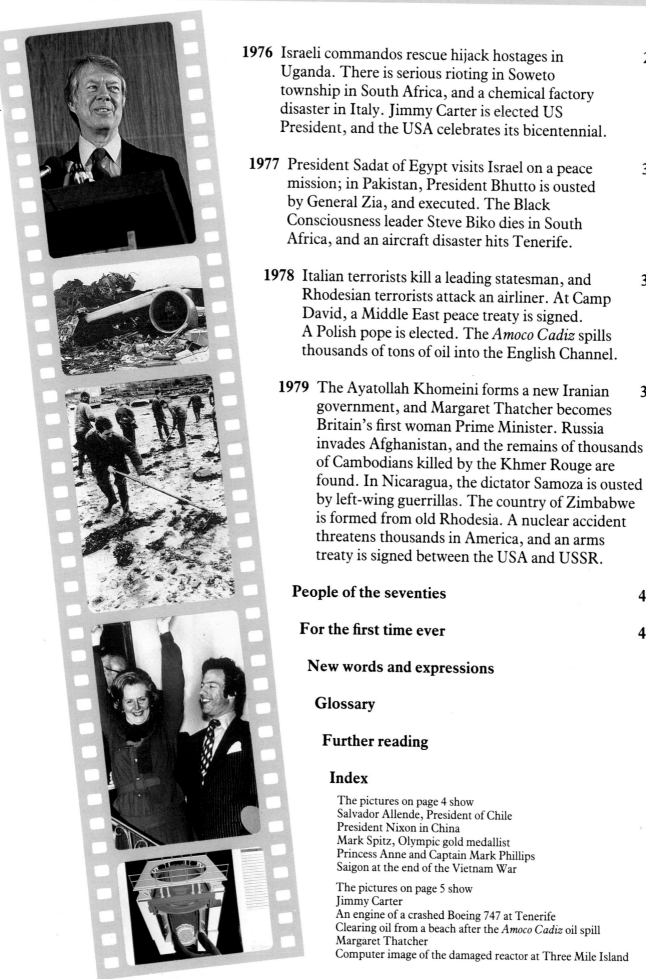

The pictures on page 4 show
Salvador Allende, President of Chile
President Nixon in China
Mark Spitz, Olympic gold medallist
Princess Anne and Captain Mark Phillips
Saigon at the end of the Vietnam War

The pictures on page 5 show
Jimmy Carter
An engine of a crashed Boeing 747 at Tenerife
Clearing oil from a beach after the *Amoco Cadiz* oil spill
Margaret Thatcher
Computer image of the damaged reactor at Three Mile Island

Introduction

The seventies was a decade of violence and disappointment. During the sixties, there had been prosperity, protest and the vision of a better future. During the seventies, hopes were dashed. The dreams of a glorious future vanished. The reality to be faced was grim, turbulent and inglorious.

The key event of the seventies was the Israeli victory in the 1973 Arab-Israeli war. In retaliation, Arab countries raised the price of oil. The result was an economic crisis from which the world had not fully recovered in the early 1990s. The age of cheap energy was over. In industrialized countries, especially the USA, people had to face higher prices for fuel. The cost of living went up.

Other wars also made the headlines. The Vietnam War ended, and smaller wars erupted in Africa, in Asia, and on Cyprus.

Revolutions often made the news. A series of dictators and dynasties were overthrown. In some cases, the uprisings had the genuine support of the people. Some were engineered by one of the two superpowers.

Russia and America continued to dominate world politics during the seventies, but other nations also grew stronger. Communist China was allowed to join the United Nations, which cleared the way for it to become a possible third superpower. At the end of the decade, another force emerged: that of militant Islamic fundamentalism.

The great plague of the seventies was terrorism; no country was completely safe from terrorist activity. Hundreds of 'political' groups tried to change the world through simple-minded violence. Their weapons included letter bombs and the hijack. Their victims were usually innocent members of the public.

Advances in communications technology made the terrorists' task easier. They wanted publicity, and millions could see on their TV screens the masked and gloating terrorists, and helpless, frightened hostages.

The seventies were also a time of great technological progress. Machines from earth landed on the two nearest planets. Orbiting laboratories circled the earth in space. Closer to home, digital watches, pocket calculators and home computers all made their first appearance.

YEARS	WORLD AFFAIRS
1970	Cambodia becomes the Khmer Republic Quebec wants to separate from Canada
1971	China joins UN Idi Amin seizes power in Uganda Federation of Arab Republics formed Malta elects socialist government
1972	British government imposes direct rule on Northern Ireland Ceylon becomes Sri Lanka
1973	Arabs raise oil prices Britain works a 3-day week 'Cod War' between Iceland and Britain
1974	President Nixon resigns India tests atom bomb
1975	Portugal grants independence to Angola Socialists win election in Portugal
1976	Jimmy Carter elected US President
1977	President Sadat visits Israel
1978	Camp David peace talks
1979	Ayatollah Khomeini returns to Iran Russia invades Afghanistan Rhodesia becomes Zimbabwe

WARS & CIVIL DISORDER	PEOPLE	EVENTS
Palestinian terrorists hijack aircraft Nigerian civil war ends US students riot over Cambodia	Salvador Allende elected in Chile Anwar Sadat elected in Egypt Janis Joplin, rock singer, dies Charles de Gaulle dies	First heart pacemaker fitted Cyclone hits East Pakistan

Pakistani army crushes rebels
India battles with Pakistan over
   Bangladeshi independence
	Calley convicted of Mylai massacre
	Three Soviet cosmonauts killed
	'Papa Doc' Duvalier of Haiti dies
	Louis Armstrong dies
		Britain goes decimal
		Britain to join Common Market
		UN elects Kurt Waldheim as Secretary-
		   General

Palestinian terrorists attack at Olympic
   Games
British army attacks Irish
   demonstrators
	President Nixon is re-elected in USA
	Bobby Fischer wins world chess title
	John Edgar Hoover dies
		President Nixon visits China
		Baader-Meinhof gang leaders captured
		Mark Spitz wins seven Olympic gold
		   medals
		Russian probe lands on Venus

Israel wins Yom Kippur War Last US troops leave Vietnam Violent coup in Chile Military coup in Greece	Nixon accused of Watergate cover-up Lyndon B. Johnson dies Pablo Picasso dies Princess Anne marries Mark Phillips	Britain joins the EEC Perón elected in Argentina Skylab repaired in space Thalidomide settlement
Turks invade Cyprus Military coup in Portugal Revolution in Ethiopia Irish violence spreads to the Republic	Patty Hearst joins in bank raid Alexander Solzhenitsyn exiled from USSR Mikhail Baryshnikov, dancer, defects	Labour wins UK election Abba win Eurovision Song Contest
Cambodia falls to the Khmer Rouge Saigon falls to North Vietnam Civil War in Lebanon Terrorists seize OPEC delegates	King Faisal of Saudi Arabia assassinated General Franco dies	Helsinki accords signed 1975 is International Women's Year Chinese clay army discovered
Commando raid rescues hostages in Uganda Riots in Soweto; schoolchildren killed	Chairman Mao dies Bjorn Borg wins at Wimbledon	Chemical factory disaster in Italy Montreal Olympic Games US bicentennial celebrations *Viking* probe finds no life on Mars
General Zia seizes power in Pakistan	Steve Biko dies in S. African police cells Elvis Presley dies Freddie Laker launches Skytrain	Queen Elizabeth's Silver Jubilee Punk rock and fashions hit Britain *Star Wars* thrills audiences

Italian Red Brigade assassinates
   Alberto Moro
Rhodesian terrorists shoot down
   airliner
	Pope John Paul II elected
	Muhammad Ali regains heavyweight
	   boxing title
		Mass suicide of People's Temple
		   members
		Amoco Cadiz disaster
		The world's first test-tube baby is
		   born

Sandanista guerrillas oust Samoza from Nicaragua Uprising in Uganda; Idi Amin flees	Mrs. Thatcher leads Conservatives Lord Mountbatten killed by IRA Pope John Paul II visits Poland	Three Mile Island nuclear accident SALT-2 treaty signed

1970

Jan 12   Nigerian civil war ends
May 4   US students shot during demonstration
Sept 12   Palestinians blow up hijacked aircraft
Sept 30   Governments give in to hijackers' demands
Oct 5   Sadat becomes President of Egypt

BIAFRA DEFEATED
NIGERIAN CIVIL WAR ENDS

Jan 12, Lagos, Nigeria The 30-month civil war ended today. The rebel province of Biafra has surrendered to the federal government. Bitter fighting continued right up until yesterday's final assault by government troops. The rebel leader, General Ojukwu, is believed to have fled to the Ivory Coast.

People in the southern province of Biafra have suffered terribly during the war. In many districts thousands of people are now starving.

During the Biafran War, refugees have received some food aid. These children line up for high-protein food made of corn, soya and powdered milk.

AMERICAN STUDENTS SHOT DEAD

May 4, Ohio, USA National Guardsmen today shot and killed four students at Kent State University. The students were demonstrating against the US invasion of Cambodia. The National Guardsmen had automatic rifles and opened fire without warning. At least one of the dead students was not taking part in the demonstration. She was walking between classes when she was hit by a bullet.

CHILE GETS MARXIST LEADER

Sept 4, Santiago, Chile Salvador Allende was inaugurated today as President of Chile. He becomes the world's first Marxist leader to be freely elected. Allende won the election despite strong opposition, which was funded by American companies operating in Chile. These companies fear that Allende's government will nationalize their profitable businesses.

HIJACKED AIRCRAFT BLOWN UP

Sept 12, Dawson's Field, Jordan Palestinian gunmen today blew up three jet airliners which they had hijacked. The empty aircraft were parked at a disused desert airstrip, Dawson's Field. The three jets (one American, one British, and one Swiss) were hijacked over Europe six days ago.

The hijackers have released most of the passengers and crew from the three jets, but some have been taken hostage. About 50 passengers are being held at a secret location in Jordan. In return for freeing the hostages, the hijackers want the release of Palestinian terrorists held in European jails.

SADAT NEW EGYPTIAN LEADER

Oct 5, Cairo, Egypt Anwar Sadat today became President of Egypt. Sadat takes over from Jamal Abd al-Nasser who died on September 28. Nasser was a very popular leader. He was revered throughout the Arab world for his tough stand over the nationalization of the Suez Canal in 1956. Nasser's death was deeply mourned in all Arab countries.

GOVERNMENTS RELEASE TERRORISTS

Sept 30, London Tonight the Swiss, British and West German governments released seven Palestinian terrorists in return for hijacked airline passengers. Among those released was Leila Khaled, who was held in Britain following a failed hijack attempt on an Israeli airliner.

Many people criticize this decision to give in to the hijackers' demands. They believe that releasing prisoners in return for hostages will probably encourage further hijackings.

CAMBODIA BECOMES KHMER REPUBLIC

Oct 9, Phnom Penh, Khmer Republic Cambodia today officially became the Khmer Republic. A military coup ousted Prince Sihanouk in March this year. The new head of state is Lon Nol, the former defence minister. The new Khmer Republic claims to be neutral in the Vietnam War. However, it is anti-Communist and is friendly with the USA. Khmer is the name of the language spoken by people in this area of Indo-China.

NEWS IN BRIEF . . .

TERRORIST BOMBINGS IN USA

March, USA Terrorism in America seems to be increasing in violence. This month, a bomb factory operated by the 'Weather Underground' exploded, killing several so-called Weathermen. The organization takes its name from a line in a song by Bob Dylan. The Federal Bureau of Investigation (FBI) have a number of Weathermen on their list of ten 'most wanted' suspects.

FIRST ATOMIC PACEMAKER

July 22, London A British man made medical history today. He was the first person to be fitted with an atom-powered artificial pacemaker. The pacemaker regulates the patient's heartbeat, and runs off a tiny atomic battery. The pacemaker can be installed completely inside the patient's body.

HALF A MILLION KILLED BY CYCLONE

Nov 14, Dacca, East Pakistan A tremendous tropical storm struck East Pakistan two days ago. It has completely devastated a large part of the Ganges delta region. At least 500,000 people are believed to have been killed, most of them swept away by the devastating floodwater.

The Pakistan government is 2000 km (1242 miles) away on the other side of India. It appears unable to provide aid to the East. Unless food and medicine arrive quickly, hundreds of thousands more people will die from starvation and disease.

ROCK STAR DRUG DEATHS

Oct 4, Los Angeles, USA It has not been a good year for rock musicians. Today, the singer Janis Joplin died of a drug overdose. Joplin, born in 1943, made her name for her impassioned blues singing. Last month in London, the guitarist Jimi Hendrix choked to death while under the influence of drugs. Hendrix, an American Negro, won fame for his distinctive playing style.

Janis Joplin

TROUBLES IN CANADA

Oct 16, Montreal, Canada Prime Minister Pierre Trudeau today declared a 'state of insurrection' in Quebec. He has called in troops to the province to restore order. There has been a series of kidnappings; a Canadian minister and a British diplomat are among those who are being held. The kidnappers are separatists who want a separate, French-speaking Quebec.

DE GAULLE DIES

Nov 9, Paris General Charles de Gaulle, ex-President of France, died today of a heart attack. De Gaulle began his career during World War II, when he was leader of the Free French forces. He served as president of France from 1958 until 1969. Under de Gaulle, France refused to join the NATO alliance as a full member. He aroused the anger of many French people by allowing Algeria to become independent. There were many attempts to assassinate him, but de Gaulle died peacefully at home.

The funeral of General Charles de Gaulle at Colombey-les-deux-églises

1971

AMIN IN – OBOTE OUT

Jan 25, Kampala, Uganda   A military coup in Uganda, led by General Idi Amin, has ousted President Milton Obote. A new government has been formed, with Amin as the new head of state. Obote is believed to have escaped to Kenya. Many of his supporters have been killed by Amin's soldiers.

BRITISH MONEY GOES DECIMAL

Feb 15, London   Britain said goodbye today to the old money system of pounds, shillings and pence. From now on, we shall be using decimal money.

Under the old system, the pound was divided into 20 shillings, each of which was worth 12 pennies. A pound was therefore worth 240 pennies. Under the new system, there are only pounds and pence. The pound is simply divided into 100 pennies. A new penny is worth about two and a half old pennies.

Many people claim that 'going decimal', or decimalization, will confuse shoppers. However, the experts say that decimal money is easier to understand. Sums involving money can now be solved using decimal arithmetic. By going decimal, Britain has at last joined the rest of the world. Most countries already use decimal money.

OFFICER GUILTY OF VIETNAM MASSACRE

March 29, Georgia, USA   US Army Lieutenant William Calley was today found guilty of the murder of Vietnamese citizens. The murders took place at the village of Mylai in 1968. At least 100 unarmed men, women and children were killed by US soldiers under Calley's command. The incident has become known as the Mylai massacre.

The massacre was first reported in the newspapers in 1969. There was a public outcry, and huge demonstrations against the war. Many Americans demanded that the guilty soldiers should be brought to justice. The authorities at last gave in to public pressure, and Calley went on trial late last year.

Lt. William Calley (centre)

PAKISTAN ARMY CRUSHES REBELS

April, East Pakistan For the last month, government troops have been attacking rebels of the Bangladesh independence movement. Thousands of civilians have been killed by the shelling of towns and cities. The independence movement in East Pakistan follows last year's cyclone. The Pakistani government failed to send enough aid. The violence used by the Pakistani army has surprised everyone. As many as a million refugees are now trying to cross the border into India. The Indian government has protested to Pakistan over the brutal way they put down the rebellion.

FEDERATION OF ARAB REPUBLICS FORMED

April 18, Cairo, Egypt Egypt, Syria and Libya are to merge to form a Federation of Arab Republics. The three countries will agree on a single constitution later this year. In the past, relations between them have not always been friendly. However, they are united by a common language and a common hatred for Israel. A vote of all the people is expected to show widespread support for the new federation.

East Pakistan refugees pack into a small open boat for the river crossing to India and safety.

MALTA GOES SOCIALIST

June 17, Valletta, Malta In a surprise result, the socialists have won the Maltese election. The new leader of this small Mediterranean island is Dom Mintoff, known for his outspoken anti-British views. A left-wing government will strain the traditional good relations Malta has with Britain. Many Maltese extremists want to shut down Britain's naval bases on the island.

BRITAIN TO JOIN COMMON MARKET

July 14, London The British Parliament yesterday voted in favour of Britain joining the Common Market. Some MPs still worry that membership will have harmful effects on British farming and fishing industries.

The Common Market is more properly called the European Economic Community (EEC). At present there are six members – France, Italy, West Germany, Belgium, Luxemburg and the Netherlands – which are sometimes known as the Six.

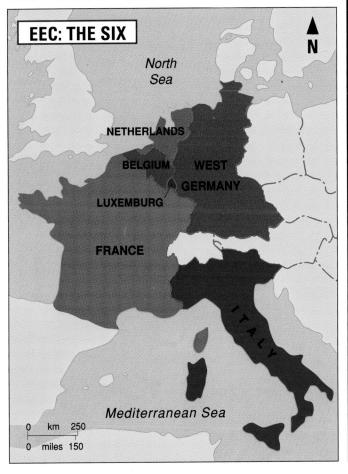

EEC: THE SIX

North Sea

NETHERLANDS

BELGIUM   WEST
          GERMANY
LUXEMBURG

FRANCE

ITALY

Mediterranean Sea

0   km   250
0   miles   150

PENTAGON PAPERS PUBLISHED

June 30, New York Two weeks ago, an American newspaper published top secret documents about the Vietnam War. On June 13, the *New York Times* published extracts from secret Pentagon research papers. These so-called 'Pentagon Papers' were leaked to the press by Daniel Ellsberg, former US Deputy Defence Secretary. Ellsberg claims that he was frustrated by the slow progress of the war in Vietnam.

The appearance of secret documents in a Sunday newspaper caused a storm of protest from the US government. Ellsberg was arrested, and the authorities tried to ban the publication of further extracts. Today, the Supreme Court of the United States ruled that newspapers were free to publish what they chose. The first amendment to the US Constitution guarantees the freedom of the press.

RED CHINA JOINS UN

Oct 25, New York The United Nations today voted to admit Communist China and expel Nationalist China (Taiwan). The Nationalist Chinese lost the Civil War to the Communists and set up their own state of China on the island of Formosa in 1949. They refused to recognize the Communist state in mainland China. The United States has in the past used its veto to keep Communist China out of the UN. The US finally gave in to the pressure of world opinion. The final vote was 76–35 in favour of allowing the People's Republic of China to join the United Nations. A Taiwan ambassador, Dr. Sampson Shen, has said this is a day of "indescribable sadness".

INDIA WINS WAR

Dec 18, Delhi, India Two weeks of bitter warfare ended in victory for India today. Pakistan has accepted India's terms for a ceasefire. Fighting broke out because India supported the rebel state of Bangladesh, formerly East Pakistan. India officially recognizes Bangladesh. The Pakistani army has been defeated. It seems now that Bangladesh will become an independent nation.

NEWS IN BRIEF . . .

VOODOO ISLAND DICTATOR DIES

April 21, Port au Prince, Haiti Haiti's much-feared dictator Dr. François 'Papa Doc' Duvalier died today of natural causes. For years, Duvalier ruthlessly held on to power by crushing all opposition. Especially feared were his hired gunmen, the 'Tontons Macoutes'. Some of his supporters also used voodoo rites to frighten the local population. Duvalier is succeeded by his son Claude, who is known as 'Baby Doc'.

COURT CLEARS MUHAMMAD ALI

June 28, Washington DC, USA The world heavyweight boxing champion, Muhammad Ali, has been cleared of avoiding military service, or 'dodging the draft'. The Supreme Court of the United States said that Ali refused to fight in Vietnam because of his religious beliefs.

TRAGIC DEATH OF THREE RUSSIAN COSMONAUTS

June 30, Moscow The Russian news agency Tass made a tragic announcement today. Three cosmonauts on the latest Soyuz mission were found dead when their capsule landed in Central Asia. They were Georgi Dobrovolski, Vladislav Volkov and Viktor Patseyev. Earlier, the cosmonauts had successfully docked their spacecraft with the orbiting Salyut space station. They are said to have been alive when they started their re-entry into the earth's atmosphere. The cause of their death has not been made public.

The Russian cosmonauts died on board a Soyuz spacecraft like this one, which made a successful 17-day flight one year ago.

CHRISTMAS FIRE KILLS 150

Dec 25, Seoul, South Korea A Christmas Day fire at a multi-storey hotel has left 156 people dead. Most of the victims were tourists who had come for the holiday. Foreign experts have blamed the high death toll on poor fire regulations in the South Korean capital. International airlines have threatened to stop all flights to Seoul unless stricter fire regulations are imposed.

LOUIS ARMSTRONG DIES

July 6, New York Jazz musician Louis Armstrong died here today aged 71. Armstrong made his name as a singer, as well as a trumpet player. He appeared in several Hollywood films, and will be best remembered for his hit version of 'Hello Dolly'.

AUSTRIAN TO HEAD UN

Dec 21, New York The Austrian diplomat Dr. Kurt Waldheim has been appointed the new Secretary-General of the United Nations. Waldheim will serve for ten years.

1972

ARMY KILLS IRISH DEMONSTRATORS

Jan 30, Londonderry, Northern Ireland British Army troops opened fire on a Catholic civil rights march and killed 13 unarmed civilians. This is the worst incident of violence since the army was first sent to Northern Ireland three years ago. There have been several previous reports of the army using excessive force. After this latest incident, many people are demanding that the troops be sent back to mainland Britain.

NIXON VISITS CHINA

Feb 21, Beijing, China President Richard Nixon today became the first US leader to visit Communist China. Until last year, America was a supporter of Nationalist China (Taiwan), and refused to recognize Communist China.

President Nixon's visit is very important for both countries. If the planned talks go well, they could lead to considerable trade between China and America. There could also be an alliance against Russia, which both see as a potential enemy.

President Nixon (right) on the Great Wall of China

15

DIRECT RULE FOR ULSTER

March 25, London The British government has imposed direct rule on the troubled province of Ulster (Northern Ireland). After more than 50 years of semi-independence, Northern Ireland will once again be ruled from London. Recent events, such as the bloodshed on January 30 which has become known as 'Bloody Sunday', have left the government with no choice. Already the government has taken power to imprison without trial anyone suspected of violent crime. Increasing violence between Catholics and Protestants threatens to bring the province to a standstill. The government has to look after the majority of the Ulster population who are not involved in the sectarian violence.

GERMAN POLICE CAPTURE TERRORISTS

June 16, Hanover, West Germany West German police have rounded up the leaders of the Red Army Faction. These terrrorists are often known as the Baader-Meinhof gang, after its two leaders, Andreas Baader and Ulrike Meinhof. Their aim is to overthrow capitalist society by violence. Their bombings, bank raids and kidnappings have left at least four dead and dozens injured.

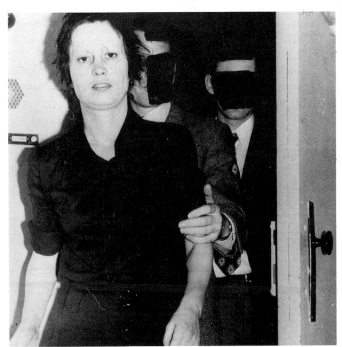

Ulrike Meinhof at her arrest

CEYLON BECOMES SRI LANKA

May 22, Colombo, Sri Lanka The island of Ceylon has become an independent republic. Formerly a part of India, the new state is to be known as Sri Lanka, which means 'great and beautiful island'.

15 KILLED IN OLYMPIC SHOOT-OUT

Sept 5, Munich, West Germany The peaceful spirit of the Munich Olympic Games was today shattered by gunfire. The trouble began when Palestinian terrorists attacked Israeli athletes in the Olympic village. Two Israelis were killed, and another nine were taken hostage. The terrorists demanded that all Arab prisoners be freed from Israeli jails in return for the release of the hostages. The German government then set a trap for the terrorists and offered them a helicopter to make their getaway. When the terrorists came out, the German police opened fire. In the gun battle that followed, all nine hostages, along with five terrorists and a policeman, were killed.

OLYMPIC ATTACK SURVIVOR SPEAKS

Sept 6, Munich ". . . a burst of shots was fired through the door. A few minutes later, another Israeli in a second apartment heard somebody ring his doorbell. Somebody else opened the door from the inside and at once four Arabs armed with Russian Kalashnikov automatic rifles came in and ordered the Israelis out. With the Arabs was one of the trainers who was already bleeding from a shot wound in the side of his face. The Arabs forced him and the other trainers to say where the rest of the team were . . . As the Arabs ordered the people in the second apartment at gunpoint to go out . . ., one of the Israelis shouted 'Let's attack'. The Arabs, however, understood, and ordered the Israelis to leave in single file. . . ."

(Dr. Shaul Ladany, Olympic athlete, reported in *The Times*)

FIVE ARRESTED AT WATERGATE

June 17, Washington DC Five men were arrested tonight at the Watergate Hotel in downtown Washington. They were caught while breaking into the offices of the Democratic National Committee. Equipment found on the burglars suggested they meant to plant electronic 'bugs'. Clearly, somebody wanted to listen to the secret meetings of George McGovern's election campaign team. The question is, who paid the burglars?

NIXON WINS BY LANDSLIDE

Nov 7, Washington DC, USA Richard Nixon has won a second term as US President in last week's election. His opponent, the Democratic candidate George McGovern, received less than 40 per cent of the votes cast. McGovern's campaign was badly damaged by a scandal involving his running mate, Thomas Eagleton. During the campaign, the Democrats also complained of 'dirty tricks' played by Republican party supporters.

NEWS IN BRIEF . . .

DRIVING ON THE MOON

April 27, Houston Astronauts from the US *Apollo 16* mission arrived back on earth today. They have been exploring the mountains of the moon in their lunar rover. This vehicle has electric motors and can climb the sides of moon craters and hills, despite the thick moon dust. The astronauts have been using the lunar rover to explore the region around their landing site in the moon's Descartes uplands.

FBI CHIEF DIES

May 2, Washington DC John Edgar Hoover, the director of the Federal Bureau of Investigation (FBI), has died aged 77. Hoover made his name during the 1930s when, in an attempt to clean up American society, he led his 'G-men' (Government Men) against gangsters. In later years, Hoover turned his attention to the so-called 'Red Menace' of Communism. As head of the FBI, Hoover kept secret files on many Americans, including film stars, politicians and even presidents.

QUEUES FOR KING TUT

June 30, London The biggest attraction in London this summer is an exhibition of treasures from the tomb of the ancient Egyptian pharoah, Tutankhamun. The tomb was discovered in the 1920s, and most of the golden treasures are usually kept at Cairo Museum.

THE SURFACE OF VENUS

July 27, Moscow The Russian space probe, *Venera 10*, today made a successful soft-landing on Venus. Because of the crushing pressures and intense heat, the probe only worked for 53 minutes.

FISCHER NEW CHESS CHAMPION

Sept 1, Reykjavik, Iceland The American player Bobby Fischer has become the new world chess champion. He beat the defending world champion, the Russian Boris Spassky. Fischer was a child prodigy and a world class player in his teens.

SEVEN GOLDS FOR SPITZ

Sept, Munich, West Germany American swimmer Mark Spitz, aged 22, won seven gold medals at this year's Olympic Games. No one has ever won more Olympic golds at a single games. Each of Spitz's victories set a new world record.

1973

March 29   US troops leave Vietnam
Sept 11   Military coup in Chile
Oct 17   OPEC raises oil price
Oct 26   Victory for Israel in Middle East war
Dec 17   Three-day working week in Britain

BRITAIN JOINS EEC

Jan 1, Brussels, Belgium   Britain, Ireland and Denmark have become members of the European Economic Community. The Six are now the Nine. In Britain, although there may be long-term benefits, there will certainly be short-term price rises. British shoppers will no longer be able to buy dairy products and meat from Commonwealth countries at subsidized prices. This may have serious effects on farming in Commonwealth countries such as New Zealand.

ARABS USE OIL PRICE AS A WEAPON

Oct 17, Vienna, Austria   The Arab oil-producing states have raised the world price of oil by 70 per cent. The announcement was made at a meeting of OPEC (Organization of Petroleum Exporting Countries). The price rise is aimed at the countries who are supporting Israel in the Middle East war. It will damage the economies of the industrial countries. Western Europe imports 80 per cent of its oil from the Middle East, and will be badly affected.

In a separate move, Arab states also announced an oil embargo against the USA. Saudi Arabia, Kuwait and other Arab oil producers will no longer sell oil to America. This is because President Nixon gave two billion dollars in emergency wartime aid to Israel. Although America has other sources of oil, this latest move will hit the US economy hard.

LAST US TROOPS LEAVE VIETNAM

March 29, Saigon, South Vietnam   The last contingent of US troops left the country today. Only American civilians now remain. The US troop withdrawal was carried out under the terms of the peace treaty which ended the war. The treaty between North and South Vietnam, the USA and the Vietcong was signed in Paris on January 27.

Car fuel is rationed in America because of the oil price rise. More than 50 cars are waiting for this service station to open.

18

NIXON INVOLVED IN WATERGATE

July, Washington DC, USA The US Senate is investigating the Watergate burglary. It seems that President Nixon was involved in the cover-up operation. The Senate committee has already heard how the burglary was organized by White House aides and members of the Committee to Re-elect the President. It has now emerged that Nixon himself gave instructions for the bungled burglary to be kept quiet. All conversations in the President's office were tape recorded. The President has been told to hand all the tapes over to the investigating committee.

COD WAR DEATH

Aug 29, Reykjavik, Iceland An Icelandic naval engineer was killed today when his gunboat collided with a British Navy vessel. This is the latest incident in the 'Cod War'. Britain and Iceland are arguing over the right to fish in the seas between their two countries. Iceland has extended its fishing zone to 320 km (200 miles) off the coast. Earlier this year both sides were shooting at each other, but this is the first time someone has been killed.

Fishing vessels in Reykjavik harbour

VIOLENT COUP IN CHILE

Sept 11, Santiago, Chile President Allende of Chile has been killed during a military coup. His democratically elected government has been overthrown. The new head of state is General Pinochet, the leader of the coup. Over 2000 of Allende's supporters were killed in fierce fighting around the presidential palace. Those who survived say that the coup was organized by the American CIA, who oppose Allende's Marxist government.

PERON ELECTED IN ARGENTINA

Sept 23, Buenos Aires, Argentina Juan Perón is back in power in Argentina. The former dictator was overthrown by a military coup 18 years ago and went into exile. He returned to Argentina earlier this year to fight the elections, and was today elected President.

ANOTHER WHITE HOUSE SCANDAL

Oct 12, Washington DC US Vice-President Spiro Agnew resigned today. He had been charged with corruption and tax evasion. The scandal involving Mr. Agnew is completely separate from the Watergate affair. The charges relate to Agnew's term as Governor of Maryland. He is replaced as Vice-President by Gerald Ford.

ISRAEL WINS MIDDLE EAST WAR

Oct 26, Tel Aviv, Israel After three weeks of fierce fighting, Israel has won the war against Egypt and Syria. The United Nations has arranged a ceasefire, and UN troops are keeping the two sides apart.

The war started on October 6, the Jewish holy day of Yom Kippur. The Israelis were taken completely by surprise when Egyptian troops stormed across the Suez canal, attacking Israeli positions. To the north, Syrian troops recaptured the Golan Heights.

In response, Israeli commanders quickly organized a series of counter-attacks. By the time the ceasefire came into effect, Israel had won. The Egyptian army was surrounded in the desert, and Israeli tanks had advanced to within 30 km (18 miles) of the Syrian capital, Damascus. During the war, Israel received huge quantities of military and economic aid from the USA.

BRITAIN ON THREE-DAY WEEK

Dec 17, London British factories and offices may now only use electricity for three days a week. This is part of a package of measures designed to cope with Britain's worst economic crisis since the 1930s. The crisis has several causes. A miners' strike has cut off supplies of coal to power stations; the OPEC oil-price rise has affected the trade balance; inflation is soaring. Many experts predict that petrol will be rationed next year.

President Papadopoulos

SECOND CHANGE OF GOVERNMENT IN GREECE

Nov 25, Athens, Greece The Greek armed forces have overthrown the civilian government and seized power. This is the second change of government in Greece this year. In June the country officially became a republic under President Papadopoulos. A series of strikes and student unrest weakened his government, and today the Greek army again took control. The military first took power in the 'Colonels' Coup' of 1967.

NEWS IN BRIEF . . .

LBJ DIES

Jan 22, Texas, USA Lyndon Baines Johnson (LBJ), former president of the USA, died today of a heart attack, aged 64. Elected as Vice-President, Johnson became President when John F. Kennedy was assassinated in 1963. He was re-elected in 1964, but withdrew from the 1968 campaign. He will be remembered chiefly for America's deeper involvement in the Vietnam War during his presidency.

PICASSO DIES

April 8, Mougins, France Pablo Picasso, one of the greatest painters of the twentieth century, has died aged 91. He was born in Spain, but moved to France early in his career. Picasso was a tremendously productive artist, and painted more than 100,000 pictures. His most famous painting is *Guernica*, which portrays the horrors of the Spanish Civil War. Many people prefer the circus paintings of his 'Blue period' to his abstract, Cubist-style work.

SKYLAB REPAIRED IN SPACE

June 6, earth orbit Astronauts have repaired the damaged solar panels on Skylab, the American space station. Skylab was successfully launched last month, but when it reached orbit the solar panels were found to be faulty. Replacement panels were taken up by Skylab's crew who followed it into orbit a few days later.

THALIDOMIDE SETTLEMENT IN COURT

July 30, London A British court has awarded thalidomide victims £20 million compensation after an 11-year struggle. Thalidomide was first prescribed to women in the 1960s to relieve morning sickness during pregnancy. Some of them gave birth to babies with deformities. The court has ruled that compensation must be paid by the makers of the drug.

ROYAL MARRIAGE

Nov 14, London Princess Anne, only daughter of Queen Elizabeth II, was married today in Westminster Abbey. Her husband is Captain Mark Phillips, an army officer. An estimated 500 million people around the world enjoyed watching the ceremony on television.

1974

ARMY TAKES OVER IN PORTUGAL

April 25, Lisbon, Portugal A group of young army officers has overthrown the country's right-wing government. The officers say that their main grievance is the war in the African colony of Angola. For 13 years, Portuguese troops have been fighting guerrillas who want independence from Portugal.

The new head of state is General Spinola, a hero of the African wars. He did not organize the coup, and was invited to become leader after it had succeeded. Spinola has said that people will be free to lead their lives as usual. He has promised free elections in the near future.

INDIA GOES ATOMIC

May 18, Delhi, India India has successfully tested its first atom bomb. In doing so, India becomes the sixth country to join the atomic weapons club. Prime Minister Indira Gandhi insists that India's bombs will be used for peaceful purposes, such as mining and civil engineering.

NIXON RESIGNS UNDER PRESSURE

Aug 8, Washington DC, USA Richard Nixon has resigned the US presidency. He is the first president to do so. If Mr. Nixon had remained in office, he would have faced impeachment proceedings for his part in the Watergate scandal. Impeachment is a legal method of charging the president with crimes.

Mr. Nixon has tried hard to hide the truth about his role in the Watergate affair. The US Supreme Court has ruled that he must hand over the tapes that may prove him guilty. Rather than do that, Mr. Nixon has chosen to resign.

The new President of the USA is Gerald Ford, who became Vice-President last year.

FORD PARDONS NIXON

Sept 8, Washington DC US President Gerald Ford has pardoned ex-President Richard Nixon for any crimes that he may have committed whilst in office. As a result, Mr. Nixon no longer faces prosecution for his role in the Watergate affair. Many people believe that the pardon is part of a secret deal between Mr. Nixon and his former Vice-President.

TURKISH VICTORY IN CYPRUS

Aug 15, Nicosia, Cyprus Turkish troops today entered Famagusta, the main port and tourist centre. Since invading Cyprus on July 20, the Turkish army has made steady progress and has captured about half the island. Cyprus is now cut in two, with the Turkish army occupying the north-eastern sector.

Cyprus became independent from Britain in 1961. Since then, the Greek and Turkish islanders have often fought over land. Last month, Greek National Guard officers staged a coup, and set up an extreme anti-Turkish government. The new government wanted Cyprus to become part of Greece. In response, Turkey invaded, and there has been bitter fighting.

Turkish troops in northern Cyprus

LABOUR WINS UK ELECTION

Oct 11, London The Labour Party, under Mr. Harold Wilson, has won its second general election this year. In May, Labour failed to win a majority in the House of Commons. Today, they were re-elected with a majority of just three seats. This is not a large enough majority to make an effective government. Britain is suffering the worst economic crisis for 40 years. There have been strikes and violence on picket lines. Many ordinary citizens fear a total breakdown of law and order.

REVOLUTION IN ETHIOPIA

Sept 2, Addis Ababa, Ethiopia Haile Selassie is no longer the ruler of Ethiopia. He has been overthrown by a military coup, led by Communists.

Haile Selassie was crowned Emperor, King of Kings, Lion of Judah in 1930. He has ruled ever since then, apart from a short period during the Italian invasion of the 1930s. At first he was seen as a progressive ruler, but he is now considered a champion of conservatism. In the West Indies, he is revered by members of a sect called Rastafarians. 'Ras Tafari Makonnen' is Selassie's Ethiopian title.

Emperor Haile Selassie (left) has been deposed.

NEWS IN BRIEF . . .

SWEDISH SINGING SUCCESS

April 6, Brighton In a surprise result, the Swedish pop group Abba has won the Eurovision Song Contest with 'Waterloo'. Sweden does not have a reputation for good pop music, and has never won before in the contest's 18-year history. This year, however, the Swedes have astounded their critics. Abba's upbeat, tuneful sound has every sign of being a long-lasting success.

SOLZHENITSYN EXILED

Feb 14, Moscow, USSR The author Alexander Solzhenitsyn has been exiled from his native Russia. The Soviet authorities have taken this action in response to the publication of his new book, *The Gulag Archipelago*. This describes the terrible conditions inside Russian labour camps.

KIDNAPPED HEIRESS IN BANK RAID

April 15, San Francisco, USA Patty Hearst, the missing newspaper heiress, has been photographed taking part in a bank robbery. Miss Hearst is the daugher of newspaper tycoon Randolph Hearst. She was kidnapped in February of this year by members of a terrorist group calling themselves the Symbionese Liberation Army (SLA). They have extreme left-wing political aims. It now looks as though Patty Hearst has joined her captors, and become a member of the SLA.

An armed woman, thought to be Miss Hurst

IRISH VIOLENCE SPREADS

May 17, Dublin, Republic of Ireland The violence in Ulster has spilled over the border. Three car bombs today exploded in Dublin city centre, killing at least 20, and injuring hundreds. This is the first major terrorist attack in the Irish Republic. The bombs are believed to have been planted by Protestant extremists from Ulster.

SCHMIDT REPLACES BRANDT

May 6, Bonn, West Germany Willy Brandt has resigned as Chancellor of West Germany. He will be replaced by Helmut Schmidt. Brandt resigned after an East German spy was discovered working in his office.

SOVIET DANCER DEFECTS TO WEST

June 30, Toronto, Canada A leading Soviet ballet dancer, Mikhail Baryshnikov, defected to the West last night. He was dancing with the Bolshoi ballet company which is on tour here.

1975

SAUDI KING KILLED

March 25, Riyadh, Saudi Arabia   King Faisal of Saudi Arabia has been assassinated by a member of his own family. The murder of this moderate leader has sent shock waves throughout the Arab world. There is now expected to be a struggle for power in Saudi Arabia.

On one side of the debate are the moderates who favour rapid development. On the other side are the extremists who want to protect Islamic religious values. Few details of the struggle are expected to emerge, because the affairs of the Saudi monarchy are cloaked in secrecy.

KHMER ROUGE TAKE CAMBODIA

April 16, Phnom Penh, Cambodia   The government of the Khmer Republic, once Cambodia, has surrendered to the Communist rebels. The Communist Khmer Rouge (the 'Red Khmers') have been besieging the capital, Phnom Penh, for more than three months. Conditions in Phnom Penh are said to be desperate, with many people on the verge of starvation. At least a quarter of a million people have been killed during the five-year guerrilla war. During the war, Lon Nol was helped by American and South Vietnamese forces. There are fears that thousands more will die if the Khmer Rouge begin revenge killings.

It is not yet clear who is to be the new head of state. The most likely candidate is Pol Pot, the leader of the Khmer Rouge. However, for the time being, the exiled Prince Sihanouk continues to represent the country abroad. The Khmer Rouge will re-name the country Democratic Kampuchea.

SOCIALISTS WIN IN PORTUGAL

April 25, Lisbon, Portugal   The Socialists have swept into power in Portugal. The result came in the first free elections for 50 years. Under their leader, Mario Soares, the Socialists gained nearly half the votes cast. The moderate Popular Democrats came second, and the Communists finished a poor third.

SAIGON FALLS TO NORTH VIETNAMESE

April 30, Ho Chi Minh City, Vietnam   The Vietnam war is finally over. North Vietnamese troops have captured Saigon, the capital of South Vietnam. Saigon is to be renamed Ho Chi Minh City, in honour of the North Vietnamese leader.

There were scenes of chaos at the American embassy, as helicopters evacuated US diplomats and other foreigners. An American journalist said, "There was only one way inside: through the crowd and over the ten-foot wall. Once we moved into that seething mass we ceased to be correspondents. We were only men fighting for our lives, scratching, clawing, pushing even closer to that wall." Fights broke out as crowds of South Vietnamese tried to force their way on to the last helicopters. They fear reprisals will be taken against them by the North Vietnamese.

The North Vietnam Army (NVA) has advanced rapidly since launching an offensive earlier in the year. Without US troops to assist them, the South Vietnamese have been defeated in a series of battles. When NVA tanks rumbled into Saigon, they met almost no resistance. The South Vietnamese army had run away. Many soldiers changed into civilian clothes in order to evade capture.

HUMAN RIGHTS PACT SIGNED

Aug 1, Helsinki, Finland Leaders of 37 countries today signed a security pact after two years of difficult negotiations. The 'Helsinki accords' were signed by all the European countries, Canada, the USA and the USSR. In return for recognition of Russian supremacy in Eastern Europe, the Russians have pledged to respect and uphold basic human rights. The Helsinki accords have been hailed as a major step in the process of *détente* between Russia and America. It is hoped that the two power blocs can exist peacefully side by side, despite their differences.

WOMEN SHOOT AT FORD

Sept 30, California US President Gerald Ford has survived two separate attempts by women to kill him. On September 5, a 26-year-old with a violent past tried to shoot the President. Her gun failed to fire. On September 23, another woman fired at Ford, but her aim was deflected by a Marine guard. Both would-be assassins have been arrested.

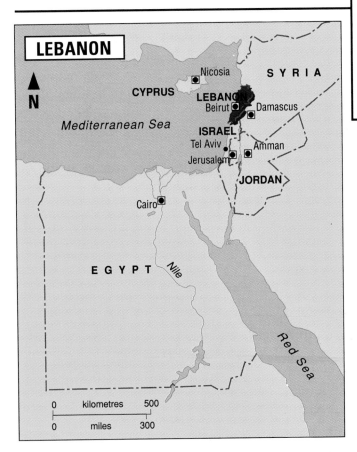

GENERAL FRANCO DIES

Nov 20, Madrid, Spain The Spanish right-wing dictator, General Franco, has died of a heart attack. Franco had ruled Spain since 1936, when he seized power at the beginning of the Spanish Civil War. Spain will now be headed by a monarch. The new leader is King Juan Carlos.

King Juan Carlos of Spain and Queen Sophia

WOMAN LEADS TORY PARTY

Feb 28, London After two ballots, the British Conservative party has elected Mrs. Margaret Thatcher, 49, to lead them. She replaces Mr. Ted Heath.

CIVIL WAR IN LEBANON

Sept 16, Beirut, Lebanon Clashes between Christian and Muslim militias have turned into full-scale civil war. The most serious fighting has been in the Arab quarters of Beirut, which have been pounded by mortar bombs and rockets. Night and day, the city streets resound with the rattle of gunfire. At least 50 people have so far been killed.

Lebanon is bitterly divided by religion and politics. The Christian minority tend to have right-wing views. The Muslim majority (which includes a great many Palestinian refugees) tend to be left-wing. Fighting first broke out earlier this year when 27 Palestinians were massacred by right-wing gunmen.

PORTUGAL QUITS AFRICA

Nov 10, Luanda, Angola Portugal today granted independence to Angola, its last African colony. In June of this year, Mozambique, Portugal's other African colony, also became independent.

Independence has put an end to the 13-year colonial war between Portuguese troops and Angolan freedom fighters. But few people believe that it will bring peace. Fighting is now expected to break out between the opposing groups of guerrillas. There are already rumours that Russia will send 'military advisers' to assist the Marxist MPLA (People's Movement for the Liberation of Angola). The other two groups, the FNLA (National Angolan Liberation Front) and UNITA (National Union for the Total Liberation of Angola), already receive some support from the West.

Members of the UNITA movement in Angola clean their weapons. The guerrilla war continues.

TERRORISTS SEIZE DELEGATES

Dec 21, Vienna, Austria Terrorists have seized more than 60 delegates to a conference of OPEC (the Organization of Petroleum Exporting Countries). Among those being held are 11 oil ministers. The terrorists are supporters of Palestine, and are led by a Venezuelan killer known as Carlos. The terrorists have already killed a policeman and a security guard. They are demanding an aeroplane in which to escape with their hostages.

Delegates at the OPEC conference

SEX EQUALITY LAWS

Dec 29, London Two new laws come into effect today. They are the Sex Discrimination Act and the Equal Pay Act. It will now be against the law to discriminate on the grounds of sex alone in jobs, education and training. Men and women doing the same job will have to be paid the same rate.

These two new laws are meant to improve the status of women in society. Many campaigners in the women's movement have been influenced by the writer Germaine Greer. Her book *The Female Eunuch* shows how women are often second-class citizens in a society ruled by men.

Today's new laws will help women work on equal terms with men, though there is still inequality in pensions, taxes and social security benefits. Many careers are still closed to women.

DOCKING FOR DETENTE

July 19, Space A joint American-Russian space link-up ended today. The US *Apollo* and Soviet *Soyuz* craft went their separate ways. Soon both will land back on earth. The flight is part of a policy of *détente* between the superpowers, and was agreed on back in 1972. The link-up was shown on TV in both countries.

NEWS IN BRIEF . . .

1975 – WOMEN'S YEAR

Jan 1, New York 1975 is to be International Women's Year (IWY), according to the United Nations. The aim is to draw attention to the many ways in which women are exploited. Several countries have legislation planned to coincide with IWY.

BRITISH ECONOMY WORSENS

June 13, London Inflation in Britain has reached 25 per cent per year. In British schools, the economics textbooks describe 25 per cent inflation as catastrophic. The books say that such inflation is only found in unstable economies such as those in South America. As prices in the shops rise, millions of British people are finding food more and more expensive.

NORTH SEA OIL FLOWS

June 18, Scotland Britain's first North Sea oil came ashore today to a Scottish refinery. The oil comes from the Argyll field, about 300 km (180 miles) out at sea. This first shipment came ashore by tanker. Later this year, the first North Sea pipeline will be opened, bringing oil direct from offshore fields.

TREE BLIGHT SWEEPS COUNTRY

Oct 30, England A fungal disease called Dutch Elm Disease has already killed 6.5 million trees in England, according to a report out today from the Forestry Commission.

CLAY ARMY DISCOVERED

July, Beijing, China Archaeologists in China have discovered a 6000-strong army of life-sized statues. Modelled in terracotta, each statue represents a soldier of the Chinese army. The statues were made about 2200 years ago. They were buried at the tomb of the first emperor, Ch'in Shih Huang Ti, who died in 206 BC.

CB RADIO CRAZE

Aug 31, New York Citizen's Band (CB) radio has become a national craze. Millions of Americans are now talking to each other by radio. The number of licences issued has trebled this year. Part of the attraction is that CB radio can be fitted in vehicles. This makes it very popular with truck drivers and other long-distance road users. CB users have imaginative call-signs or 'handles'. Among the voices you can hear on the American airwaves are 'The Lone Ranger', 'Big Momma' and 'Captain Midnight'.

Some of the first clay statues of soldiers to be unearthed

SHARK SCARES MILLIONS

Nov 21, London A film about a shark has become a world-wide hit. *Jaws* is by young American film maker Stephen Spielberg. It has been thrilling audiences from Hong Kong to Helsinki, and opened in London today. The film tells the story of a great white shark that develops a taste for human flesh, and terrorizes a popular holiday resort.

1976

RIOTING IN SOWETO

June 16, Johannesburg, South Africa   Serious rioting is taking place in the black township of Soweto, near Johannesburg. The police have been firing live ammunition into crowds of black people. At least 50 people are reported killed, and hundreds have been wounded.

Demonstrations and rioting broke out following a government decision that the language Afrikaans must be used in black schools. For the blacks here, Afrikaans, a form of Dutch, is the hated language of the extremist white minority. Many black schoolchildren have been taking part in strikes, marches and demonstrations. Children as young as 12 have been killed by police bullets, and hundreds have been arrested.

June 17, Soweto   "When I visited Soweto this afternoon a thick pall of smoke caused by tear gas and burning vehicles hung over a small hill where the riot was taking place. Two army helicopters made repeated sorties over the riot area as reinforcements of armed police moved there. Eyewitnesses said the helicopters were dropping tear gas canisters . . .

"The mood of the inhabitants was very hostile toward all whites. At Orlando police station two women were dragged away by the police for shouting 'Kill the whites'. As I drove to the riot area a car full of Africans waved me down and warned me that if I went any farther I would be killed by rioting students."   (Nicholas Ashford, in *The Times*)

ISRAEL RESCUES HOSTAGES IN UGANDA

July 4, Entebbe, Uganda In a daring raid, Israeli commandos have rescued 110 hostages that were being held at Entebbe airport. The hostages had been taken prisoner when their airliner was hijacked a week ago over Greece. The hijackers then flew to Uganda where President Idi Amin offered to help them.

The commandos were flown the 4000 km (2480 miles) from Israel and landed secretly by night. The raid was a success, although three of the hostages were killed by gunfire in the battle at the airport. All seven terrorists, five Palestinians and two Germans, died in a hail of bullets. One Israeli soldier was killed. Before flying the hostages back to Israel, the commandos also destroyed 11 Ugandan jet fighters.

President Amin is said to be outraged by the Israeli attack. His support for the hijackers will have damaged his reputation among world leaders.

CHEMICAL DISASTER IN ITALY

July 10, Soveso, Italy An explosion at a weedkiller factory has released poisonous gas over an Italian town. Among the chemicals involved is dioxin, which is deadly even in very small amounts. The town of Soveso could stay contaminated for years.

Bodies of dead animals are removed by scientists wearing decontamination clothing.

OLYMPIC BOYCOTT DOES NOT SPOIL THE GAMES

Aug 2, Montreal, Canada Most African nations boycotted the Olympic Games at Montreal, which ended today. The boycott was in protest that New Zealand took part in the games. New Zealand still plays some sports with South Africa.

Despite the boycott, the games were a great success. Star of the summer was 14-year-old Nadia Comaneci, the Romanian gymnast, who won three gold medals. Nadia made Olympic history by being the first competitor ever to receive a perfect maximum score of 10.0.

CHAIRMAN MAO DIES

Sept 2, Beijing, China Chairman Mao Tse-tung has died aged 82. Mao had been China's leader since 1949, when he led the Communist revolution. The whole country is making a show of national grief. Behind the scenes there is certain to be a power struggle for the leadership of China. Among likely contenders are the radical 'Gang of Four', who are led by Chairman Mao's widow.

CARTER ELECTED PRESIDENT

Nov 2, Washington DC James (Jimmy) Carter is to be the new US President. The rival candidate was Gerald Ford. The contest between them was fierce, and Carter won today's election by only a narrow margin. The new Vice-President is to be Walter Mondale.

Mr. Jimmy Carter and his wife Rosalynn and family at the election victory

NEWS IN BRIEF . . .

BOWIE FILM DEBUT

March 19, Hollywood, USA Rock star David Bowie has been given his first starring role in a major film. In *The Man Who Fell To Earth*, Bowie plays a mysterious scientific genius from another planet. Unlike other pop stars who have gone into movies, Bowie will not be singing in his film.

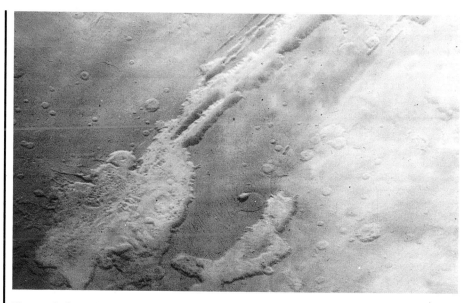

Part of the giant Valles Marineris canyon system on Mars, photographed from *Viking 1*

BJORN BORG WINS WIMBLEDON

July 3, London Bjorn Borg has become the first Swede to win the men's singles championship. Borg, who is 21, beat the Romanian Ilie Nastase in three straight sets. Borg is a very popular champion; he is polite but cool on the tennis court. The long-haired player has attracted the same sort of following as a pop star.

NO LIFE ON MARS

Aug, Mars The US *Viking 1* planetary probe has not found life on Mars. Last month *Viking* became the first probe to land successfully on Mars. Photographs of the planet's surface showed a red, barren world. As well as cameras, *Viking* carried equipment for three separate experiments designed to answer the old question: is there life on Mars? Scientists are still arguing about the results. So far, they admit they have found no evidence of it.

USA BICENTENNIAL CELEBRATIONS

July 4, USA Today, people all over the United States are celebrating the country's bicentennial. It is the two hundredth anniversary of the Declaration of Independence. From coast to coast, every town and city has special events planned. Nearly everyone is going to a party. Tonight, hundreds of millions of fireworks will light up the sky. Tomorrow, the fun will be over and once again the country will go back to worrying about the energy crisis and other economic problems.

SUMMER DROUGHT IN BRITAIN

Aug 25, London Britain is having its hottest, driest summer on record. Over most of the country, there has been no rain for three months. Reservoirs are drying up. In parts of southern England, there are plans to ration water if it does not rain soon. Meanwhile, the government has today created a Minister for Drought, Mr. Dennis Howell. He has announced severe penalties for those using hose pipes to wash cars or to water their dried-up gardens.

ARABS EYE ANTARCTIC ICE

Sept 30, Riyadh, Saudi Arabia The Saudi government is looking at a strange idea which may solve its water problems. This desert country has one-third of the world's oil, but is desperately short of fresh water. Under the new proposal, icebergs would be towed from near the South Pole, and anchored off the Saudi coast. As the icebergs melted, fresh water would be collected and piped ashore. The water from each iceberg would cost about 100 million US dollars.

1977

WORLD'S WORST AIR CRASH

March 27, Tenerife, Canary Islands   The world's worst aircraft disaster has killed 574 people. The accident involved two Boeing 747 jumbo jets. They were packed with European and American holiday-makers. One of the aircraft was about to take off, and full of fuel, when it collided with the other on the runway. Both aircraft went up in a ball of flame. First reports say there are more than 70 survivors. Their escape must be something of a miracle.

Wreckage of aircraft at Tenerife airport

DUTCH MARINES STORM HOSTAGE TRAIN

June 11, Amsterdam, The Netherlands   Dutch commandos today fought a gun battle with South Moluccan terrorists. The terrorists come from a former Dutch colony which is now part of Indonesia. Cover was provided by smoke bombs dropped by jet fighters. The terrorists were holding hostages, many of them passengers on a train that was seized by the South Moluccans three weeks ago. Others were teachers and pupils at a local school. Six terrorists and two hostages were killed in the gun battle. Nine terrorists were arrested.

GENERAL ZIA SEIZES POWER

July 5, Islamabad, Pakistan   General Zia ul-Huq, the chief of the Pakistani army, has taken control of the country. President Ali Bhutto has been arrested and is being kept under armed guard.

The military coup follows several months of civil unrest in Pakistan. Many people accused Mr. Bhutto of corruption and of cheating in the last elections. He leads the Pakistan People's Party. Pakistan has been under martial law since April of this year. Today, General Zia took that military control one stage further, and made himself head of state. There are fears for Mr. Bhutto's life.

PANAMA CANAL TO BE PANAMANIAN

Sept 6, Panama City   Since it was completed in 1914, the Panama Canal has been owned by America. Under a new treaty signed today, the canal will belong to the Republic of Panama in 1999. The treaty was signed by US President Jimmy Carter, and Panama's President Torrijos. The treaty is very popular in Panama. But at home in the USA, President Carter has been accused of giving away the country's assets.

SADAT VISITS ISRAEL

Nov 18, Tel Aviv, Israel   President Sadat of Egypt has made history as the first Arab leader to visit Israel. He comes on a mission of peace, and he was welcomed by the Israeli President, Menachem Begin.

Sadat's visit could mark the start of a new era in Middle East politics. This is the first time that the two sides in the Arab-Israeli conflict have met for talks. The two leaders will discuss the problem of Palestine, and the Israeli occupation of the West Bank of the Jordan.

President Sadat has declared that he wants a permanent peace for all the Arab countries. However, several Arab leaders have condemned his visit. They have denounced President Sadat as a traitor to the Arab cause.

Menachem Begin, Anwar Sadat and Moshe Dayan

THOUSANDS ATTEND BIKO FUNERAL

Sept 25, Pretoria, South Africa   More than 15,000 people attended the funeral of Steve Biko, a leading black activist. Biko died in mysterious circumstances on September 12, while he was in police custody. His supporters have accused the police of murdering Biko, and claim that his body was covered with bruises. The police deny any responsibility and say that he died of natural causes. Biko's death has sparked off a series of demonstrations, some of them violent. More than a thousand blacks have been arrested during the last two weeks.

NEWS IN BRIEF . . .

GARY GILMORE EXECUTED

Jan 17, Utah, USA The murderer Gary Gilmore has been executed by firing squad. He was sentenced to death for two murders. Gilmore is the first American in ten years to suffer the death penalty. His execution marks a victory for those who have been campaigning for a return to capital punishment.

YOUTH GOES PUNK

June 21, London A new fashion has emerged among British teenagers. The new look is called punk. Elements of punk include: spiky hair dyed bright colours, white pancake make-up and torn clothing. The look is created out of whatever materials come to hand. For example, safety-pins are worn as earrings.

Punk also has its own sound. Punk rock records have been rising high in the charts. The music centres around a very loud, fast, driving beat. The lyrics are often used to shock the audience. One punk group, The Sex Pistols, makes a point of being extremely offensive. Their song 'God Save the Queen' was today banned from British TV.

BRITAIN CELEBRATES QUEEN'S JUBILEE

June 6, London Lines of bonfires lit up the sky tonight, as Britain starts a week of official and less formal celebrations. Her Majesty Queen Elizabeth II has been on the throne for 25 years, and her subjects are celebrating a traditional Silver Jubilee. There will be street parties in towns and cities all over Britain.

Fans of Elvis Presley gather at the singer's funeral in Memphis.

ELVIS 'THE KING' DIES

Aug 16, Memphis, Tennessee Elvis Presley, 'the King of Rock'n Roll', has died of a suspected drug overdose at the age of 46. Presley first hit the charts in 1956, and has been making hit records ever since.

CHEAP AIR TICKETS

Sept 26, London The Skytrain service takes off today. Passengers from London to New York will fly for about one-third the normal price. These cheap flights are the idea of British businessman Freddie Laker. By keeping costs down, he can pass the savings on to the passengers. The travelling public love the idea of Skytrain, but there is strong opposition from many of the other airlines.

STAR WARS THRILLS MILLIONS

Dec 28, London The hit movie of the year is *Star Wars*, which opens in London today. This highly polished science fiction adventure is filled with believable hardware and astonishing special effects. The film has brought old-fashioned fun back to the cinema. Behind all the space-age gadgetry, *Star Wars* is a simple story about rescuing a captured princess.

Harrison Ford as Han Solo, and Carrie Fisher as Princess Leia in a scene from *Star Wars*

1978

MORO MURDERED BY RED BRIGADE

May 9, Rome, Italy The body of Italian statesman Alberto Moro was found in a car boot today. Moro was kidnapped by Red Brigade terrorists two months ago, and was being held hostage. Members of the Red Brigade are Communists who want to destroy capitalist society. The terrorists wanted some of their jailed comrades to be released. The Italian authorities had refused to negotiate for Moro's life.

The Moro kidnapping has had a tremendous impact in Italy. Italians have grown used to minor Red Brigade activity; they are no longer surprised by attacks on politicians or businessmen. But Moro was someone special; he was five times prime minister, and held the respect of the nation. The police have promised to try even harder to track down and smash the Red Brigades.

RHODESIAN AIRLINER SHOT DOWN

Sept 4, Salisbury, Rhodesia Terrorists have shot down a Rhodesian civil airliner in a remote part of the country. Some 18 people survived the crash, but ten of them were later machine-gunned to death. It seems that the terrorists are members of the Patriotic Front. These guerrilla fighters are trained by Cubans. They are at war with the white minority government of Prime Minister Ian Smith.

MIDDLE EAST PEACE TALKS IN USA

Sept 18, Camp David, USA President Sadat of Egypt has agreed terms for a comprehensive peace treaty with President Begin of Israel. Agreement was reached only after intense diplomacy by US President Jimmy Carter, who is the host of the peace talks.

President Sadat (left), President Carter and President Begin

THIRD POPE THIS YEAR

Oct 16, Vatican City, Italy   A Polish priest has become the first non-Italian pope for more than 400 years. Cardinal Karol Wojtyla today became Pope John Paul II. He chose the name in honour of his predecessor, John Paul I, who died last month. John Paul I was a very popular pope, but he died after only 33 days in office. Before this, Pope Paul VI had reigned from 1963 to his death in August this year.

OIL SPILL ON FRENCH COAST

March 24, Brittany, France   The supertanker *Amoco Cadiz* has spilled 250,000 tons of oil into the English Channel. The ship broke apart after drifting onto rocks in stormy weather. A huge floating oil slick has formed. It has already polluted more than 100 km (62 miles) of the French coastline. Holiday beaches are covered with sticky crude oil, and the local fishing industry has been devastated. The French government has said there will be a massive clean-up.

NEWS IN BRIEF . . .

CULT COMMITS MASS SUICIDE

Nov 29, Jonestown, Guyana The bodies of 913 members of a religious cult have been found at an isolated jungle temple. The dead showed signs of cyanide poisoning. Police also found the bodies of five American investigators, who had been murdered. The police believe that on September 18 the leader of the cult, Jim Jones, murdered the five investigators. The next evening he mixed cyanide into a drink and commanded his followers to commit suicide with him.

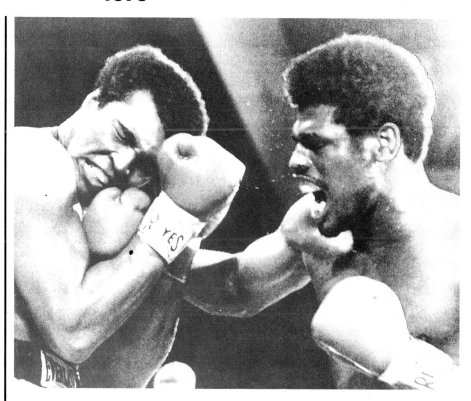

Ali (left) and Spinks

BRITAIN TO EXPORT OIL

June 27, London British North Sea oil production is now more than one million barrels per day. (One barrel is 159 litres.) Britain now ranks 16th in the list of world oil producing nations. Within two years, the country will be self-sufficient in oil; and shortly afterwards, Britain will begin to export oil.

BABY GIRL MAKES HISTORY

July 26, Manchester, England Today baby Louise Brown was born to delighted parents. She is the world's first 'test-tube baby'. An ovum from her mother and sperm from her father were mixed in a test-tube, then placed in the mother's uterus. The pregnancy was normal. The doctor in charge is Patrick Steptoe.

ALI WINS CHAMPIONSHIP AGAIN

Sept 17, New Orleans, USA Muhammad Ali has regained the world heavyweight boxing championship title by beating Leon Spinks. Earlier this year, Spinks beat Ali and won the championship. Last night, Ali proved that he is one of the greatest boxers of all time. He won the world title for a record third time.

EUROPEANS WIN AT WIMBLEDON

July 8, London A young Czechoslovakian player, Martina Navratilova, has won the ladies' tennis championship. The Czech girl beat last year's champion, Chris Evert of the USA.

In the men's finals today, Bjorn Borg of Sweden won his third consecutive title. Not since the 1930s has a player won the men's championship for three years in a row.

Martina Navratilova and her trophy

NO MORE LITTLE RED BOOK

Oct 29, Beijing, China The authorities here have denounced the 'little red book', which contains the sayings of Chairman Mao. Every Chinese citizen had to have a copy when Mao was in power. For a time, it was the best-selling book in the world. The book has now been condemned for encouraging a personality cult around the former Chinese leader. Last year the radical 'Gang of Four', led by Mao's widow, was imprisoned.

1979

Feb 1   Ayatollah Khomeini is new leader of Iran
May 4   Mrs. Thatcher is elected in Britain
July 20   Sandinista rebels overthrow Nicaraguan dictator
Nov 4   US embassy and hostages seized in Tehran
Dec 25   Russia invades Afghanistan

ISLAMIC REVOLUTION IN IRAN

Feb 1, Tehran, Iran The Ayatollah Khomeini returned to Iran today to form a new Islamic government. He replaces the Shah of Iran. The Shah fled the country two weeks ago, when he was faced with massive demonstrations in support of Khomeini.

The elderly Ayatollah (a religious title) has been living in exile in Paris. He is an Islamic fundamentalist, and is bitterly opposed to the Shah's attempts to modernize Iran. It is expected that Khomeini will abolish many of the Shah's reforms, and impose a strict religious government.

The foreign policy of the new government remains a mystery. Khomeini is known to be strongly anti-American, because the USA supported the Shah. Equally, he is bitterly opposed to Communism because of its atheism. Most observers believe that the new regime will lead to greater instability in the Middle East.

NUCLEAR ACCIDENT IN AMERICA

March 29, Pennsylvania, USA An accident at the Three Mile Island nuclear power station is threatening thousands of people who live nearby. A failure in the cooling system has caused the nuclear reactor to overheat. The authorities say that the danger of explosion is now past, but there is still a small risk of radioactivity escaping. People living within three kilometres (one and a half miles) of the power station are being evacuated.

DANGER RISES NEAR THREE MILE ISLAND

Pennsylvania, USA "I keep a Geiger counter behind my desk. This time I pulled it out and took a reading right there in my chair. It didn't read much, but it was slightly more than I would have expected . . . I took the counter down to my car and started the drive to Three Mile Island. Our office is on the far side of Harrisburg, sixteen miles from the power plant, and as I drove through the city, I saw the radiation level slowly start to rise. That pretty much told me that the level I was reading came from the reactor. Driving east, the meter rose until it stopped at three or four millirems. I looked around and found myself parked right next to the plant."

(Tom Gerusky, head of Pennsylvania's Bureau of Radiological Protection, quoted in *Three Mile Island*, Mark Stephens, Junction Books 1980)

AMIN FLEES UGANDA

March 29, Kampala, Uganda Idi Amin has been forced to flee from the Ugandan capital, Kampala. Despite help from Libyan troops, his forces have been defeated by rebels supported by Tanzania. Amin is believed to be organizing a last stand in the north of the country. Amin has presided over a regime marked by tribal bloodshed and murder.

THATCHER FIRST WOMAN PRIME MINISTER

May 4, London Margaret Thatcher has been elected Prime Minister, and becomes the first woman in Britain to hold this office.

Mrs. Thatcher became leader of the Conservative party in 1975. She is well known for her outspoken views, especially about Britain's membership of the Common Market. Now that the Conservatives are back in power, people will look to Mrs. Thatcher to lead Britain out of its economic crisis.

SALT-2 TREATY SIGNED

June 18, Vienna, Austria Russia and America have agreed to limit the number of nuclear missiles they both hold. President Leonid Brezhnev of the USSR and US President Jimmy Carter today signed the SALT-2 treaty. Under the treaty, the two superpowers are limited to a maximum of 2250 missiles each. President Carter described the treaty as 'a victory in the battle for peace'.

SANDINISTAS OUST SAMOZA

July 20, Managua, Nicaragua Left-wing Sandinista guerrillas have finally won the long battle against the government forces. The Nicaraguan dictator, General Samoza, has resigned and flown into exile. If the Sandinistas manage to form a government, they face a tough struggle in rebuilding the country. The guerrilla war that ousted Samoza has killed thousands, and left one-fifth of the population homeless.

POL POT WAS MASS MURDERER

July 30, Phnom Penh, Cambodia The new government here has accused Pol Pot of killing more than three million citizens. Pol Pot was overthrown earlier this year when Vietnam invaded and defeated the Khmer Rouge forces. Evidence has emerged that Pol Pot followed a campaign of genocide against the Cambodian people. Huge piles of human skulls have been found.

Skeletons from mass graves are kept at a Buddhist temple as a memorial to the victims of the Pol Pot regime.

A worker wearing a radiation suit, at the entrance to the damaged nuclear reactor

MOUNTBATTEN KILLED BY IRA

Aug 27, Dublin, Ireland   Lord Mountbatten has been killed by an IRA bomb whilst on a fishing holiday in Ireland. Mountbatten was a cousin of Queen Elizabeth II, and served as the last viceroy of India before independence in 1947. Lord Mountbatten was the IRA's second major target for murder this year. In March, the Conservative MP Airey Neave was killed by a car bomb in London.

The IRA bomb killed Lord Mountbatten, third from left in this holiday photo.

STUDENTS SEIZE US EMBASSY

Nov 4, Tehran, Iran   Fanatical student supporters of the Ayatollah Khomeini have captured the US embassy here. They have taken hostage nearly 100 of the American staff.

For several weeks the students have been holding anti-American demonstrations outside the embassy. They believe that America has been plotting against Ayatollah Khomeini, Iran's new leader. Today, the students climbed the embassy walls, and took over the building by force.

Soviet soldiers in Afghanistan

RHODESIA TO BE ZIMBABWE

Dec 21, London   An agreement signed in London today has ended the guerrilla war in Rhodesia. It also ends 14 years of illegal rule by a white minority government. The former British colony is to become the independent nation of Zimbabwe. Free elections, open to both blacks and whites, will be held to choose the new government. The elections are expected to be a contest between the rival guerrilla leaders Robert Mugabe and Joshua Nkomo. In the meantime an interim government will be headed by Bishop Muzorewa.

RUSSIA INVADES AFGHANISTAN

Dec 25, Kabul, Afghanistan   Russian tanks today crossed the border of Afghanistan in a full-scale invasion. Yesterday, Soviet commandos shot the leader of the Afghan government, and seized the country's main airport. Russian aircraft are now flying in thousands of troops and tons of heavy equipment.

The unprovoked invasion of Afghanistan has been condemned all over the world. The Russians, however, say the Afghans asked them for 'aid and assistance'.

NEWS IN BRIEF . . .

SID VICIOUS TAKES DRUG OVERDOSE

Feb 2, New York Sid Vicious, ex-member of the Sex Pistols punk group, today died of a heroin overdose. Last year, Vicious was arrested for the drug-related murder of his girlfriend Nancy Spungen, but released on bail.

SPACE PROBE NEAR JUPITER

March 7, Space The US space probe *Voyager 1* has sent pictures back to earth. They reveal that the planet Jupiter has a ring around it. Like Saturn's rings, it is composed of rocky debris and is 28 km (18 miles) thick.

A man is winched down to one of the wrecked Fastnet yachts.

POPE VISITS POLAND

June 2, Warsaw, Poland Pope John Paul II became the first pope to visit a Communist country for more than 30 years. It is an emotional visit, both for the Polish-born Pope, and for the millions of Polish Catholics. More than two million people lined the streets of Warsaw to welcome him.

YACHT RACE DISASTER

Aug 15, London At least 25 yachts taking place in the Fastnet Race have been sunk during three days of fierce storms. Over 100 crew members have been rescued, but 14 are reported drowned. The Fastnet Race is held every other year. Yachts sail between the coasts of Ireland and England.

NOBEL PRIZE FOR MOTHER TERESA

Dec 10, Stockholm, Sweden The 1979 Nobel Peace Prize has been awarded to Mother Teresa of Calcutta. Mother Teresa has been working with the homeless and 'the poorest of the poor' in India since 1946. Her charitable work has been acclaimed around the world.

'DUKE' WAYNE DIES

June 11, Los Angeles, USA The American film star John 'Duke' Wayne has died here of cancer aged 72. Wayne was known chiefly for his roles in westerns such as *Stagecoach* and *True Grit*. To many cinema-goers he was the typical American male: tall, strong, tough-talking, and with a heart of gold. In private life, Wayne was noted for his right-wing political views.

PEOPLE OF THE SEVENTIES

Richard Milhous Nixon, 1913-1994

Richard Nixon qualified as a lawyer before entering politics in the 1940s. During the 1950s he served as Vice-President under Eisenhower. In 1960 he stood for the presidency, but was defeated by John Kennedy. He was elected President in 1968, and again in 1972. He had staunch anti-Communist views and stood for self-reliance. He opened relations with Communist China, and began arms limitation and trade talks with Russia. Nixon took US troops out of Vietnam. In 1974 he was forced to resign over the Watergate scandal.

Leonid Ilyich Brezhnev, 1906–1982

The son of a steelworker, Brezhnev studied at technical college and worked as a surveyor. He joined the Communist Party and made his way up the political ladder, entering the Soviet Politburo in 1952. In 1977 he was named party chairman and President. Brezhnev was the last of the old-style Russian leaders. The 'Brezhnev doctrine' was a belief in the unity of the Communist world under the leadership of the Soviet Union. He followed a policy of *détente* with the West, negotiating the SALT agreements of 1969 and 1972. However, he was not afraid to use force to protect Russian interests, as in the case of the invasion of Afghanistan.

Mother Teresa of Calcutta, 1910-1997

Born Agnes Gonxha Bojaxhiu in Albania, she decided at the age of 12 to become a missionary. She joined a sisterhood of nuns in Ireland, and later sailed to India. There she studied medicine, and started her work amongst the poorest of the poor in Calcutta, during the 1950s. By the 1970s, there was a network of 700 shelters and clinics for the desperate and dying throughout India. Her work has now spread to deprived areas all over the world. Mother Teresa has received many awards and medals, including the Nobel Peace Prize in 1979. All the prizes she has won have been used in her work.

Germaine Greer, Australian writer 1939–

Germaine Greer was born in Melbourne, and studied at Melbourne and Sydney Universities before moving to England to study at Cambridge. She lectured in the late 1960s in English at Warwick University. Her fame came with the publication of *The Female Eunuch* (1970), which was a huge best-seller. The book exposed the frustration of women in a male-dominated society. Her academic rigour was a match for all anti-feminist critics. She was hailed as a leading figure in the women's movement of the 1970s. Her later influential works include *Sex and Destiny* (1984) and *The Change* (1991).

Alexander Solzhenitsyn, Russian writer 1918–

Solzhenitsyn first became internationally famous in 1970 when he was awarded the Nobel Prize for Literature. The authorities in Russia refused to let him accept the award. In 1974, he was expelled from the USSR because of his book *The Gulag Archipelago*. It described the brutality of Russian prisons and labour camps where countless thousands of political prisoners died. Solzhenitsyn's other books include *Cancer Ward* and *One Day in the Life of Ivan Denisovich*. He moved to Switzerland after his exile, and continued to criticize the Soviet system, especially its denial of human rights. However, he has also been critical of the materialism and decadence of the West.

Henry Kissinger, 1923–

US politician and diplomat. Between 1957 and 1977, Kissinger advised six US presidents on matters of national security. He was most influential under President Nixon, and was largely responsible for the invasion of Cambodia during the Vietnam War and the withdrawal of US troops from Vietnam. He was awarded the Nobel Peace Prize in 1973.

Anwar Sadat, 1918—81

Egyptian leader. Sadat became President of Egypt following the death of Nasser in 1970. After Egypt's defeat in the 1973 war with Israel, Sadat turned his efforts towards peace. He restored relations with the West, and made a historic visit to Israel in 1977. In 1978 he negotiated the Camp David peace treaty, and was jointly awarded (with Prime Minister Begin of Israel) the Nobel Peace Prize in the same year.

Willy Brandt, 1913–1992

Chancellor of West Germany. Brandt entered politics during the immediate post-war period, and became mayor of West Berlin in 1957. In 1969 he was elected Chancellor. While in office, Brandt worked towards a more unified Europe, and he was a champion of the EEC. After his resignation, he headed the Brandt Commission. This looked at ways of redistributing wealth between the rich, industrialized countries of the North, and the poor, developing countries of the South.

Stephen Spielberg, 1947–

American film director. The most successful film director of the 1970s, Spielberg first hit the headlines with *Jaws*. Despite being made primarily for adult audiences, many of Spielberg's films display a very strong sense of the wonder and delight of childhood. His later successes include *Close Encounters of the Third Kind* and *E.T.*, both concerned with alien visitors to earth.

For the first time ever

1970	UK/USA	Jumbo jets enter service on trans-Atlantic route
	USA	Floppy disks for computers introduced
	France	Solar-powered furnace completed
1971	USA	First commercial production of microprocessors ('silicon chips')
		High pressure water jet used as cutting tool in manufacturing industry
	USA/UK	Direct dial telephone calls between New York and London
1972	USA	First feminist magazine published
	UK	CAT (Computer Aided Tomography) scanner introduced
	Holland	Laser video disk developed
1973	USA	Colour photocopiers become available
		Computer barcoding introduced in supermarkets
	UK	'Salter Duck' wave energy device invented
		A house is built that is totally self-sufficient in energy, water and sewage treatment
1974	UK	Programmable pocket calculator introduced
	Germany	Solar-powered cigarette lighter goes on sale
	Japan	Microbes used to synthesize human hormones
1975	UK	Long-life LCDs (Liquid Crystal Displays) used in calculators and clocks
		First successful cloning of a mammal (rabbit)
	USA	Home computer kits launched
	Japan	Pong, the first video game, goes on sale
	USSR	Experimental thermonuclear (fusion) power station begins operation

1976	USA	Ink-jet printers introduced
		First APPLE mini-computer built
		Legionnaires' disease identified
1977	USA	Television signals transmitted down optical fibres
		Space shuttle makes first unpowered test flight
		First man-powered flight over 1.6 km course
1978	UK	First 'test-tube baby' born (*in vitro* fertilization)
	USA	Atlantic crossed by balloon
	Japan	First auto-focussing camera goes on sale
	USSR	Three spacecraft dock in orbit (*Soyuz 26*, *Soyuz 27*, and *Salyut 6*)
1979	Japan	'Walkman' personal stereo is launched
	Canada	World's first satellite TV service

New words and expressions

The following words and phrases first came into popular use during the 1970s. Do you know what all the words mean?

Arclight	hypermarket
barcode	lifestyle
CAT scanner	LCDs
clone	neutron bomb
Common Market	preppie
debug	Provo
designer jeans	quadraphonic sound
devolution	Sensurround
digital watch	silicon chip
disco	Sloane Ranger
floppy disk	streaker
flying picket	ten-four
funk	test-tube baby
glam rock	Vietnamization
H-block	weapons system
hot pants	

Glossary

Common Market: popular term for the European Economic Community (EEC), now known as the European Community (EC), an organization dedicated to improving trade between member countries.

CIA: Central Intelligence Agency, a US government organization. The CIA has two roles: a passive role of collecting information, and an active role in attempting to overthrow governments that are hostile to the USA.

decimalization: process by which Britain changed over to a money system based on 100 pence to the pound.

détente: process through which the USA and the USSR attempted to improve relations between them.

embargo: a trade ban.

FBI: Federal Bureau of Investigation, America's national police force. The FBI deals only with serious crimes such as kidnapping, hijacking and terrorism.

genocide: systematic murder of an entire nation or race.

guerrilla: soldier who does not belong to a recognized national army. The term 'guerrilla warfare' is used to describe fighting that consists of small isolated incidents.

hijack: forcible take-over of a ship, aircraft or train.

Khmer Rouge: Communist forces from the Khmer-speaking area of Indo-China.

impeachment: formal legal process by which a serving head of state is charged with serious crimes.

IRA: Irish Republican Army, a terrorist organization which wants an end to British rule in the province of Northern Ireland.

OPEC: Organization of Petroleum Exporting Countries.

Pentagon: five-sided office building that is the headquarters of the United States military forces. The word is often used to refer to America's military leadership.

Politburo: the inner cabinet of the Russian government.

Red Brigades: Italian left-wing terrorists.

SALT: Strategic Arms Limitation Treaty. An agreement to limit the number of long-range nuclear weapons.

sectarian: belonging to a sect, or religious group.

self-sufficient: producing what a community needs within that community, rather than buying it elsewhere.

South Moluccan terrorists: Indonesian rebels demanding independence by the use of violence.

terrorist: someone who attempts to influence politics by using violence against civilians.

Ulster: another name for Northern Ireland, which is part of the United Kingdom.

veto: forbid. The power of veto is the right to refuse.

Index